How Is a Book Made?

by Grace Hansen

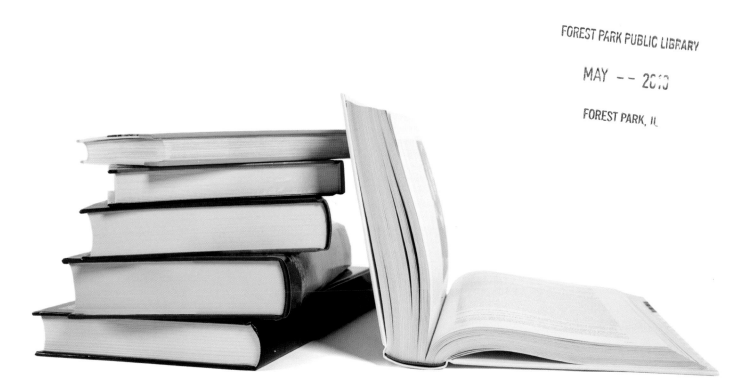

Abdo
HOW IS IT MADE?
Kids

abdopublishing.com

Published by Abdo Kids, a division of ABDO, P.O. Box 398166, Minneapolis, Minnesota 55439.

Copyright © 2018 by Abdo Consulting Group, Inc. International copyrights reserved in all countries. No part of this book may be reproduced in any form without written permission from the publisher.

Printed in the United States of America, North Mankato, Minnesota.

052017

092017

THIS BOOK CONTAINS RECYCLED MATERIALS

Photo Credits: Corporate Graphics, iStock, Science Source, Shutterstock

Production Contributors: Teddy Borth, Jennie Forsberg, Grace Hansen

Design Contributors: Dorothy Toth, Laura Mitchell

Publisher's Cataloging in Publication Data

Names: Hansen, Grace, author.

Title: How is a book made? / by Grace Hansen.

Description: Minneapolis, Minnesota : Abdo Kids, 2018 | Series: How is it made? | Includes bibliographical references and index.

Identifiers: LCCN 2016962387 | ISBN 9781532100420 (lib. bdg.) | ISBN 9781532101113 (ebook) | ISBN 9781532101663 (Read-to-me ebook)

Subjects: LCSH: Books--Juvenile literature.

Classification: DDC 686--dc23

LC record available at http://lccn.loc.gov/2016962387

Table of Contents

Making a Book

Books can be made in all shapes and sizes. Many books are printed each day.

Most books are made

using large machines. These

machines need lots of space!

First, a final **manuscript** is approved for print. The manuscript is **etched** into large plates.

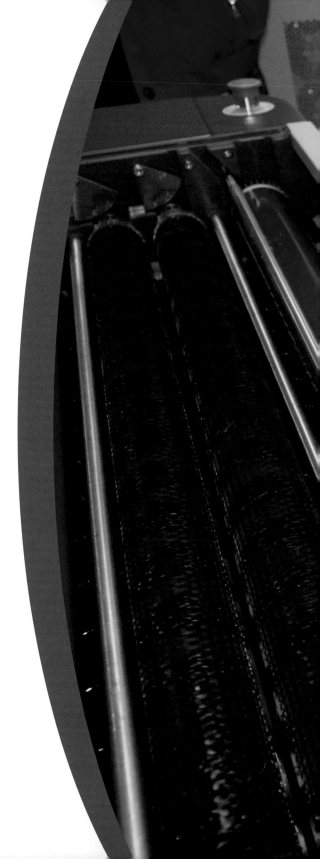

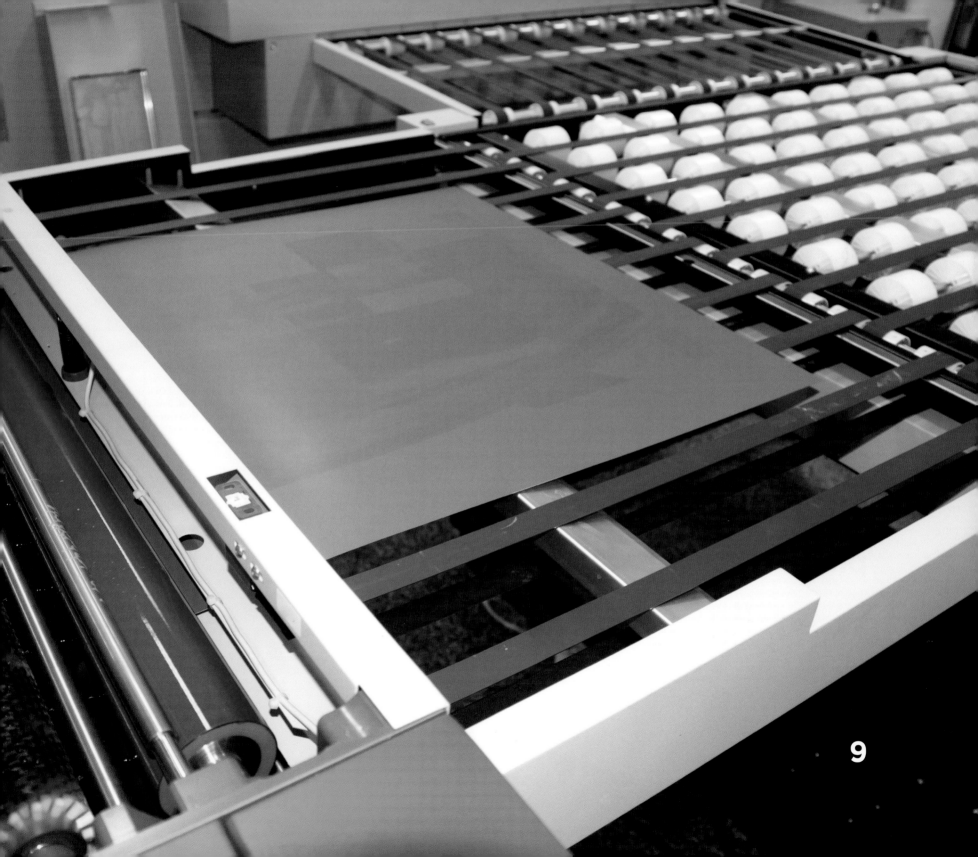

9

The plates are put into
a **printing press**. Ink is
spread over the plates.
The ink transfers from the
plate to rubber, then to paper.

paper

rubber

The large sheets are cut into smaller sheets. Then the sheets go through a folding machine. Each folded section of the book is called a signature.

The signatures are then sent
to the binding machine. They
are laid on top of each other
in order. Signatures can be
stapled, glued, or sewn together.

15

Because the pages were folded together, the books cannot open. A large steel blade cuts the folded edges.

Now the books need covers!
Covers are made on a long
printing press. Each section
of the press applies a
different color.

The Finished Product

The books then go to the **casing-in machine**. It puts glue on the book's spine. Then the hardcover and book are stuck together.

20

More Facts

- Machines bind most books today. But there are people who still bind books by hand. They are called bookbinders.

- Johannes Gutenberg was a German inventor who changed printing forever in 1440. He invented a printing press that had movable wooden or metal letters. This was the standard for a few hundred years.

- *Harry Potter and the Deathly Hallows*, the seventh and final book in the Harry Potter series, had an initial print run of 12 million copies. This was the largest initial print run in history.

Glossary

casing-in machine – a machine that attaches a book to its cover.

etch – cut or carve text or design on a surface.

manuscript – an author's text that has not yet been printed.

printing press – a machine for printing text or pictures from type or plates.

Index

abdokids.com

Use this code to log on to abdokids.com and access crafts, games, videos and more!

Abdo Kids Code:
HHK0420